Where Silence Speaks

Hearts That Hold On

Eshna

Made with ❤ on the BookLeaf Publishing Platform
www.bookleafpub.in
www.bookleafpub.com

Dedication

This collection would not be what it is without the people who have stood by me through life's ups and downs.

My family, my friends and the quiet moments that helped me find clarity have shaped every word on these pages. This dedication is my way of saying thank you—for your love, your support and the reminder that even in silence, we are never truly alone.

To my family—*You are the heart of everything I do.*
To my husband— *Thank you for being my constant. Your presence and strength make life feel steady and safe.*
To my children—*You both remind me every day of the power of unconditional love, laughter and staying true to yourself.*
To my friends—*Thank you for being there, in both the loud moments and the quiet ones.*

I am grateful to each of you for being part of my life and my story.

And to anyone who has ever found comfort in the quiet moments of self-reflection—*this is for you.*

Preface

Silence often speaks louder than anything we can say.

It holds the weight of unspoken words, the truth we
sometimes fear and the pain we quietly carry.
Silence often bears the heaviest truths. It holds
everything we long to say and everything we are too
afraid to hear.

*Silence is both an end and a beginning—a place where
words fade but meaning lingers.*
*Yet silence is also a space for healing—*a quiet refuge
where we begin to understand ourselves, accept what we
cannot change and find peace in moving forward.

This book is a collection of those quiet moments—the
ones that shape us, break us and ultimately help us grow.

These are not perfect poems but they are honest. They
capture the rawness of human emotions, showing both
the chaos of emotions and the simple beauty of being
open and real.
This is not just a personal story but a shared one—a
reminder that we all face these moments in our own
way.

While some of these words come from my own experiences they are not mine alone. They carry pieces of stories witnessed, feelings felt and moments that remain in the memory long after they have passed.

This collection is for anyone who has struggled with unspoken words and unanswered questions, for those who have ever felt lost, misunderstood or found comfort in the silent moments of self-reflection.

As you read I hope you find traces of your own story within these pages. And in doing so I hope you feel a little less alone.

Acknowledgements

Creating this collection has been a personal and thoughtful experience.

These poems came from quiet moments—times when silence held more meaning than words ever could.

I am truly thankful to everyone who has been part of this journey. To those who stood by me during uncertain times, listened without judgment and showed me that silence, though sometimes heavy, can also be healing— your presence has meant the world.

I am also grateful for the silent moments themselves—the ones that brought clarity, acceptance and the strength to keep going. Without them, these poems wouldn't exist.

To you, the reader, thank you for picking up this book. If even one line makes you feel understood or brings a little peace, then these words have done what I hoped they would.

I hope it reminds you that even in the quiet, you're never truly on your own.

1. The Fear of Goodbye

Nothing scares me more
than love that fades overnight.
One moment, you're everything,
the next, a stranger in sight.

We built something real,
or at least I thought we did.
But love that vanishes so fast
must have never truly lived.

You held me close,
then pushed me away.
I keep asking what changed,
but silence has nothing to say.
So I hold my questions tight,
pack them in my heart's embrace,
and walk away with nothing but space.

2. A Box of Sadness

At first, I asked "Why?"
but silence was all I found.
The answers never came,
just echoes all around.

Then sadness sat beside me,
wrapped its arms around my chest.
Not cruel, not loud, just patient,
never angry, just at rest.

It whispered, "This is yours now,
a weight you'll learn to bear."
I hated it, I fought it,
but it didn't really care.
And so I stopped resisting,
let it settle in its place,
until one day, I found some space.

3. My Brain is Sorry

My heart leads me blind,
chasing hope down every street.
My brain stands back and watches,
waiting for me to admit defeat.

It never shouts, never warns,
just shakes its head in doubt.
It lets me fall, lets me break,
then quietly pulls me out.

It never says, "I told you so,"
but I hear it all the same.
It patches up the damage,
but it knows I'll play again.
And when I do, it sighs,
"Go on then, love again,
but next time, don't pretend."

4. The Unseen Lines

You drew your lines in air so thin,
I never knew when I stepped in.
Your silence told me far too late,
another trap, another fate.

A forest rigged with hidden snares,
where every word I spoke was wrong.
No sign to guide me safely through,
no way to know where I belonged.

I gave you pieces of my soul,
hoping they'd light up the way.
But the deeper in I wandered,
the darker it became.

And when I turned to find you,
I found nothing left to see.
You were just a shadow, leaving me

5. Falling Apart

One card fell, then another,
but I barely even blinked.
A tower built so carefully,
gone faster than you'd think.

It wasn't one great tragedy,
not one fight, not one mistake.
It was the little things we let go,
the little ways we let it break.

A joke that wasn't funny,
a call we didn't make.
A promise left unspoken,
a silence left to take.

And then one day, the house was gone,
the foundation torn in two.
I looked around in shock—did you?

6. Forgiving Myself

I hurt for the both of us,
but you never felt a thing.
I knocked on every door,
but you never let me in.

I spoke until my voice was gone,
until my hands were bruised and sore.
I waited at your doorstep,
but you never opened the door.

And so, I took a step away,
then another, then one more.
Not because I wanted to,
but because my heart was torn.

And now I whisper to myself,
"You tried, you did your best."
And slowly, I let go of the rest.

7. Ships in the Night

We were meant to pass by,
two ships on a quiet sea.
But we threw ropes and held on tight,
as if fate had plans for you and me.

Through storms and waves we fought,
through nights so long and cold.
We thought we'd sail together,
but some journeys can't be controlled.

The ropes began to fray,
and I saw you looking far away.
You let go first—I held on still,
until my hands had nothing left to feel.

And as you disappeared from sight,
I traced the blisters on my skin,
realizing I was never meant to win.

8. Let It Hurt

I tried to push the pain away,
to bury it beneath my days.
I told myself to keep moving,
but the hurt refused to fade.

It knocked so softly first,
a whisper I could ignore.
Then louder, then stronger,
until I couldn't shut the door.

So, I sat down beside it,
let it speak, let it stay.
I cried, I listened,
I let it have its say.

And when it was done,
it let go of me too.
Not all at once—but bit by bit, it moved.

9. Half of My Heart

Some days, I don't know
how to speak to myself.
My words feel like strangers,
my voice feels like someone else.

I reach for warmth but find it gone,
I search for light but see no sun.
Half of my heart is missing,
but I'm not sure where it's gone.

Did I lose it when you left?
Did I give too much away?
Or was it never really whole,
even before that final day?

But I will keep looking,
I will find my missing part,
and when I do, I'll stitch it to my heart.

10. When Speaking Became a Sin

Every time I spoke my mind,
I became the villain in your eyes.
Every time I said, "This hurts,"
you turned away and let me cry.

I thought love meant understanding,
but I was the only one who tried.
I kept reaching, kept explaining,
while you just let the distance rise.

Loving someone is not enough
if they don't feel it in their bones.
If my words only built walls,
then maybe I was meant to go.

And so I stopped explaining,
stopped begging to be heard—
and in the silence, I found my worth.

11. The Weight of My Own Choices

Do I get to cry for the pain I made?
Do I get to curse the road I paved?
Do I get to say, "I didn't know,"
when I was the one who walked so brave?

I made the choices, step by step,
I took the turns that led me here.
And yet, when I look around,
I wonder why the path feels unclear.

But maybe blame is not the key,
not for you, and not for me.
Maybe healing means forgiving
the person I used to be.

And when I take another step,
I'll walk with wisdom, not regret.
A little lighter, not there yet.

12. The Silence Was the Answer

I wanted words to fix the pain,
I wanted answers, something clear.
I wanted one last conversation,
to understand why you weren't here.

But silence is an answer too,
even if it feels unkind.
It tells me more than words could say,
it closes doors inside my mind.

You didn't want to explain,
you didn't care to make things right.
And maybe that's the real truth—
not the words I thought I'd find.

So I stop searching for your reasons,
I stop knocking on your door.
I let your silence speak no more.

13. Between What Should Be and What Is

She stayed because she believed,
because love was meant to last.
She held on tight to what they were,
ignoring how it cracked.

She whispered, "This is worth it,"
even when it drained her dry.
She gave and gave, then gave some more,
but he never asked her why.

And then one day, she had no more,
no energy, no light.
She looked at love, but it was gone,
an echo in the night.

So she packed her heart in careful hands,
stepped away from all she knew,
and learned that leaving can save you too.

14. The Friend Who Faded

A friendship doesn't break in two,
it drifts like leaves upon the breeze.
A word unsaid, a call ignored,
a fading echo in the trees.

I reached for you, but you let go,
you slipped like sand between my hands.
Not with anger, not with blame,
just silence I don't understand.

I wonder if you even saw
how I held on until the end.
But maybe you were never mine,
not meant to be my lifelong friend.

So I send you peace, I send you love,
for what we had and what we lost.
Some things aren't meant to be held too long.

15. The Strength to Walk Away

When someone makes you feel unwanted,
don't leave to make them sad.
They won't miss what they let go,
their heart won't ache the way yours has.

Leave because your soul deserves
a place where it feels seen.
Love should not be something begged for,
it should not be a silent plea.

If they don't fight to keep you near,
then let yourself be free.
Some people are worth the effort,
some will meet you halfway through.

But if you're the only one still standing,
then there's nothing left to do.
Some love is best left in the past.

16. The Echo of What Was

Some nights, I still hear your voice,
not in words, but in the quiet.
The way laughter used to fill the air,
the way friendship felt so solid.

But now, there's just the silence,
the space where you used to be.
No anger left, no bitterness,
just memories that visit me.

I don't chase them anymore,
I let them come and go.
Some things aren't meant to stay,
some bonds aren't meant to grow.
And though I miss what once was ours,
I no longer mourn its end.

17. A Love That Never Spoke

You never told me why you left,
you never gave me words.
Just turned away and walked ahead,
like I was something burned.

I traced the past for answers,
but all I found was air.
I reached for you a thousand times,
but you were never there.

Maybe love was never love
if it only lived in me.
Maybe caring isn't real
if it makes me feel so weak.
So I write your name one final time—
and let the ink just fade.

18. The Ghost of Someone I Knew

I met you once in another life,
where we were not just strangers.
You knew my voice, I knew your thoughts,
we walked through storms together.

But somehow, time unraveled us,
like thread pulled loose from seams.
We held on tight, but lost our grip,
a shipwreck lost at sea.

And now, when I see you smile,
it's like I never knew
the way you used to say my name,
the way you saw me through.
A ghost now wears your face so well—
I guess I haunt you too.

19. The Space Between Us

There was a time you filled my world,
when I was sure of you.
Your name was written everywhere,
your love was something true.

But slowly, space crept in between,
a whisper first, then more.
A step away, a longer pause,
the silence felt unsure.

Until the space was all there was,
no words left to defend.
You drifted far, I stayed behind,
pretending it wasn't the end.
But distance speaks as loud as words—
and ours said, "We are done."

20. The Strength in Goodbye

I thought that love should fight to stay,
that leaving meant defeat.
That if I cared, I must hold on,
that giving up was weak.

But love is not a battlefield,
not something you must chase.
Not something that should drain your heart,
not something lost in space.

And so, I take a breath today,
and walk the other way.
Not bitter, not with anger's weight,
but lighter as I say—
some things aren't meant to stay with us,
and that is still okay.

21. A Love That Stays

Love is not the fleeting kind,
not hands that let you go.
Not words that turn to silence fast,
or feelings that don't grow.

Love is in the smallest things,
the laughter that we share.
The way you hold my hand so tight,
to show that you are there.

It doesn't ask for proof to stay,
it doesn't walk away.
It doesn't leave me wondering
if I should beg or pray.
It simply stays, and that's enough—
a love that's real, a love that lasts.

22. The Magic of Friendship

Some friends are written in the stars,
like maps that lead us home.
They walk beside us in the dark,
so we are not alone.

They know the words we cannot say,
they hear the thoughts unspoken.
And even when the world gets loud,
our bond remains unbroken.

No distance pulls, no time erases,
the laughter, light, and care.
For true friends live within the heart,
and love is always there.
So when I think of friends I trust,
I count you first—my dearest one.

23. The Gift of Being Known

There is no joy like being seen,
no gift like being known.
No feeling quite as warm and real,
as knowing you're not alone.

To speak your heart and hear them say,
"I know, I feel that too."
To be yourself and have them stay,
not leave when you are blue.

It's not about the perfect days,
or never feeling weak.
It's knowing that when storms arrive,
someone will hear you speak.
So if you have a love like this,
hold on—it's rare, and it is true.

24. Love Without Conditions

Love is never earned or weighed,
nor tallied like a score.
It doesn't shift with passing moods,
or ask for something more.

It holds you when you lose your way,
and calms your restless mind.
It doesn't speak in angry words
or leave your heart behind.

For love is patient, strong, and sure—
a quiet, steady grace.
It doesn't need perfection's mask,
just your unguarded face.
And when you find a love like this,
you've found life's sweetest place.

25. The Quiet Kind of Love

Love doesn't shout to prove it's real,
it doesn't need a stage.
It lives within the smallest things
that only grow with age.

It's in the cup of morning tea,
the warmth of knowing glances.
The silent strength that holds you close
when life takes backward chances.

It's in the space where words run out
but comfort lingers still—
a love that never has to ask,
yet always, always will.

26. When Love Feels Easy

Love shouldn't feel like uphill roads
or drowning while you swim.
It shouldn't weigh your spirit down
or make the light grow dim.

It feels like breathing softer air
or laughter you can't hide.
Like finding peace in someone's arms
and not the need to hide.

It meets you where your soul feels bare,
not asking you to prove—
for love, when true, feels light and clear,
like life was made to move.

27. Where Love Stands Strong

True love won't ask you to become
someone you're scared to be.
It won't disguise its heart in games
or hold you silently.

It stands beside you, steady, calm,
through sunshine and through rain.
It doesn't walk when life gets hard
or turn away from pain.

It's in the roots that never break,
the arms that never tire—
a love that stays, no matter what,
and lifts you ever higher.

28. The Peace of Being Loved

There's peace in knowing you are loved,
no need to wear a mask.
No constant worry if you're 'too much,'
no complicated task.

It's knowing that your heart is safe,
that flaws don't push away.
It's feeling seen, and held, and known
on every kind of day.

For love is not a fleeting thing,
a thrill that burns and dies—
it's peace that lingers in your soul
and never says goodbye.

www.ingramcontent.com/pod-product-compliance
Lightning Source LLC
LaVergne TN
LVHW010954200726

843509LV00013B/2415